My Little Book of
BIRDS

By Gina Ingoglia

Illustrated by Rosiland Solomon

Todd A. Culver, Education Specialist,
Cornell Laboratory of Ornithology, Consultant

A GOLDEN BOOK · NEW YORK

Western Publishing Company, Inc., Racine, Wisconsin 53404

What Is a Bird?

Birds are two-legged animals covered with feathers. They also lay eggs. There are almost nine thousand different kinds of birds, and they live all over the world—in hot deserts, leafy jungles, on frozen icebergs, and even in busy cities.

Most birds can fly. But not all of them!

Big and Little

The ostrich is the biggest bird in the world. It can grow eight feet tall and weigh over three hundred pounds. Because their wings are small compared to their large bodies, ostriches can't fly. But they can run forty miles an hour on the ground—as fast as a galloping horse.

The hummingbird is the smallest of all birds. Some are only two inches long, shorter than a thumb. The wings of a hummingbird beat so fast, they are hard to see when the bird is flying. Like a helicopter, the tiny bird can hover, or stand still in the air.

Hummingbirds use their long, thin bills to drink nectar from flowers.

A Place to Live

Most birds build nests and lay their eggs
in them. Warblers are among the many birds
that build nests in trees. The leafy branches
of the tree keep off the rain and hot sun.
After the eggs hatch, the parents bring food
to the baby birds. In less than two weeks,
the little birds can fly.

The phoebe is one kind of bird that doesn't mind living near people. Phoebes even build their nests under the roofs of porches.

Keeping Warm and Dry

Feathers protect birds by keeping their bodies warm and dry. Ducks and other water birds have a special way to waterproof their feathers. With their bills, they reach for oil that comes from a gland at the base of their tails. Then they spread the oil on their feathers. Covering themselves with this oil is called preening.

The wings of most birds are naturally waterproof. But this is not true of the double-crested cormorant. After swimming, the bird must spread its large wings to dry in the sun.

Great Swimmers

Penguins are birds that spend most of their lives in water. They have short feathers that grow close together to keep their bodies warm in icy water. Instead of wings, penguins have strong flippers. Their flippers help them dive and swim fast underwater. Penguins cannot fly.

Yearly Trips

Before cold weather comes each winter, some birds fly south to warmer climates. In the spring, they fly back north to cooler climates. These journeys are called migrations. The arctic tern migrates a grand total of 22,000 miles a year. That much traveling would almost take you around the world.

Powerful Eyes

Many birds see well, and the eagle has especially good eyesight. High in the sky, a hungry eagle searches for food by gliding on the wind with its wide wings. It can spot something on the ground to eat, such as a small animal, from a mile up in the air!

Owls hunt for food at night. They see better in the dark than most birds. With their big eyes and keen hearing, they can fly through the night and notice even the tiniest movement on the ground below. Owls can also turn their heads almost completely around—which means they sometimes seem to have eyes at the backs of their heads!

Seafood Lovers

Gulls live by the ocean and eats lots of
fish. They watch for schools of small fish by
flying above the water. Hungry gulls often
follow fishing boats out to sea and back.
There's always the chance a tasty scrap will
be tossed overboard.

Gulls also eat clams. But clam shells are hard to open. To break the shell, a gull flies into the air with a clam in its mouth and then drops it onto a rock. When the clam hits the rock, the shell cracks apart.

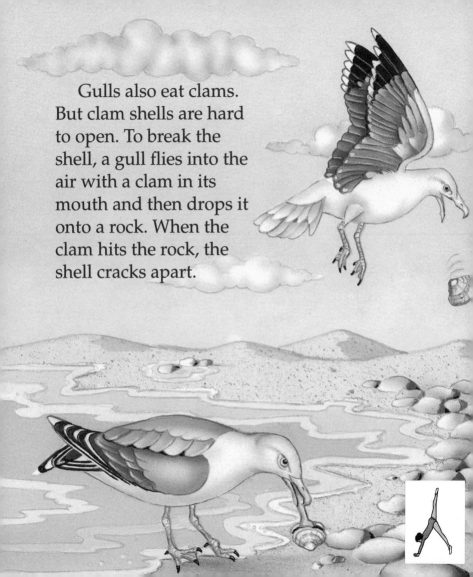

Waders

Waders are birds that find food by walking in shallow water. Their long necks and legs keep their bodies from getting wet.

Flamingos are waders. Flamingos like to feast on shrimp. They eat so many red shrimp, their feathers turn pink!

The snowy egret hunts by stirring pond bottoms with its feet. With a fast jab of its sharp beak, the bird captures darting fish or small scurrying crabs.

A Tree Climber

A woodpecker is a bird that hunts for insects under tree bark. The bird holds on to the trunk of a tree with its claws. Then it uses its beak like a drill to peck holes in the tree. Using its long tongue, the woodpecker reaches into the hole to pull out the insects.

A Fancy Bird

The male peacock is one of the most beautiful birds in the world. It has long blue-green feathers that unfold into a huge fan. The amazing pattern on the feathers looks like tiny eyes. When the fan is closed, the feathers trail behind the bird.

Curvy Necks

Another beautiful bird, the mute swan, swims with its beak pointed down and its long neck held in a graceful *S*. Needing plenty of room to take off, the large bird signals nearby swans that it is about to take flight by facing the wind and raising its long neck.

Another swimming bird, the anhinga, or snakebird, swims with only its head and snaky neck above water. When it looks for food, the bird spears a fish on its bill, tosses the fish in the air, and catches it with its open mouth.

Great Talkers

Each kind of bird has its own way of communicating. Birds sing or chirp or call out in order to scare off enemies, attract mates, or alert one another to dangers.

The mockingbird imitates the sounds of other birds. It often sings at night, when most birds are asleep.

Some birds imitate human beings and the words they speak. The best bird "talkers" have bright feathers. They are the parrot and parakeet.

Living Together

Around the world, certain kinds of birds are in danger. Pollution is making them sick. People are cutting down the trees they need for their nests.

We must change our ways. And if we make the world a better place for the birds, it will be a better place for us as well.